VOCAL SELECTIONS

An American in Paris *A New Musical*

ISBN 978-1-4950-2992-9

Cover art: Serino/Coyne

GERSHWIN® and GEORGE GERSHWIN® are registered trademarks of Gershwin Enterprises
IRA GERSHWIN™ is a trademark of Gershwin Enterprises

HAL•LEONARD® CORPORATION

7777 W. BLUEMOUND RD. P.O. BOX 13819 MILWAUKEE, WI 53213

In Australia Contact:
Hal Leonard Australia Pty. Ltd.
4 Lentara Court
Cheltenham, Victoria, 3192 Australia
Email: ausadmin@halleonard.com.au

Visit Hal Leonard Online at
www.halleonard.com

I GOT RHYTHM

Music and Lyrics by GEORGE GERSHWIN
and IRA GERSHWIN

4

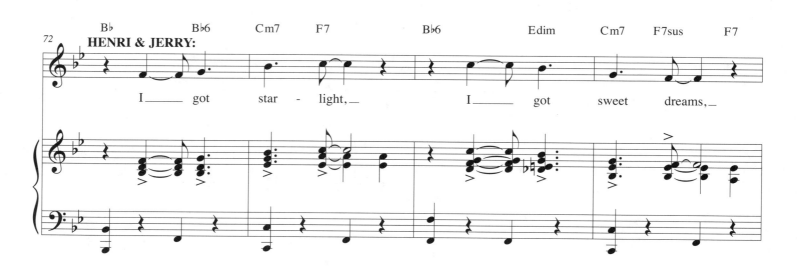

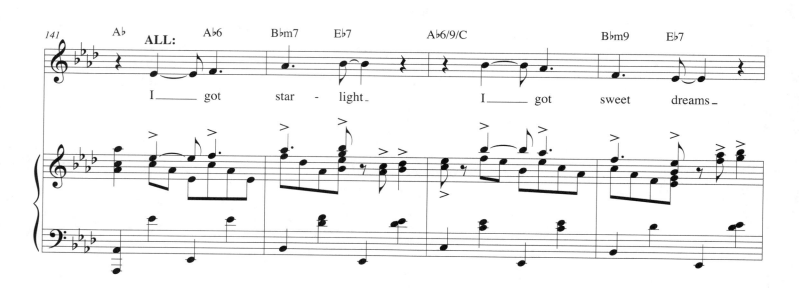

PRELUDE II

By GEORGE GERSHWIN

* Andante con moto e poco rubato (q = 88)

p legato

As presented on Broadway.

I'VE GOT BEGINNER'S LUCK

Music and Lyrics by GEORGE GERSHWIN
and IRA GERSHWIN

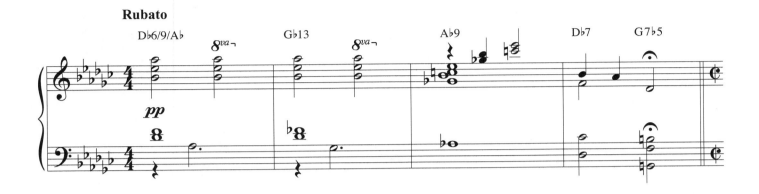

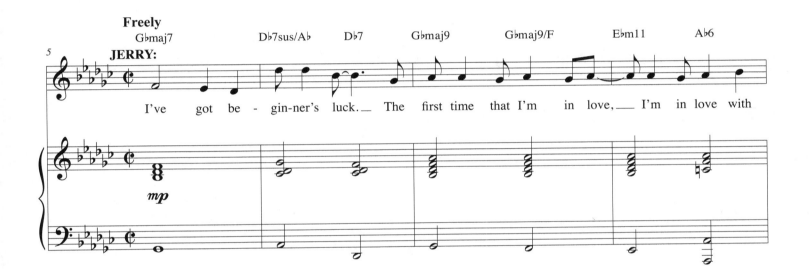

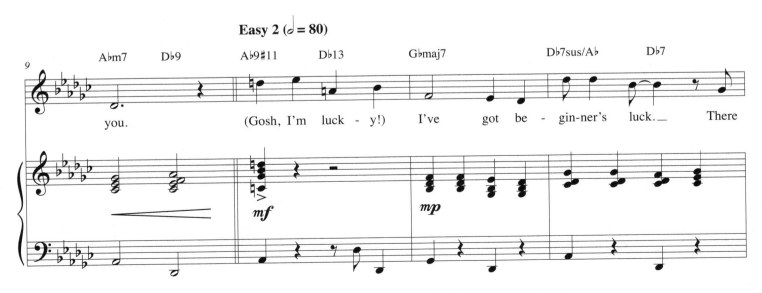

first time that I'm in love, ___ I'm in love with you. ___

'Cause

I've got be - gin-ner's luck, ___ Luck - y through and

THE MAN I LOVE

Music and Lyrics by GEORGE GERSHWIN
and IRA GERSHWIN

Moderato, simply

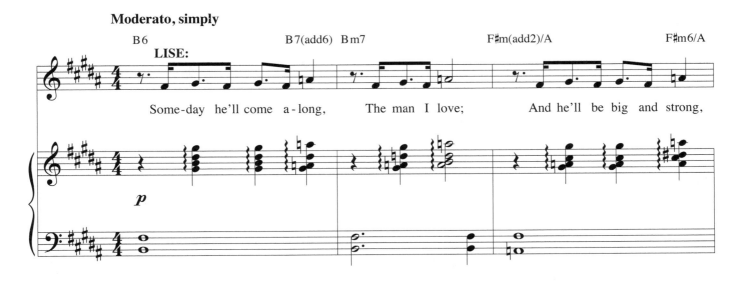

LIZA
(All the Clouds'll Roll Away)

Music by GEORGE GERSHWIN
Lyrics by IRA GERSHWIN and GUS KAHN

'S WONDERFUL

Music and Lyrics by GEORGE GERSHWIN
and IRA GERSHWIN

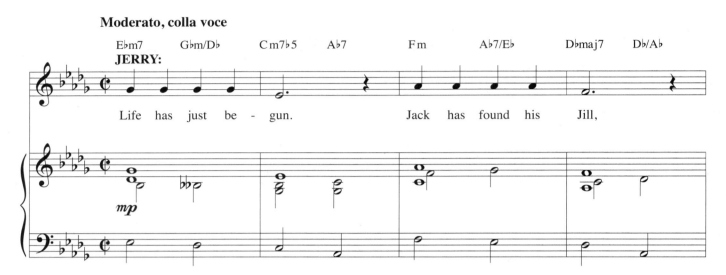

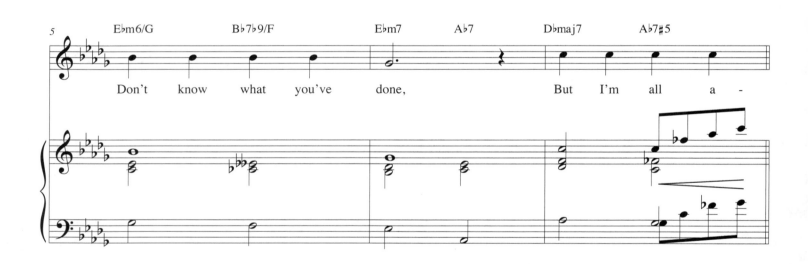

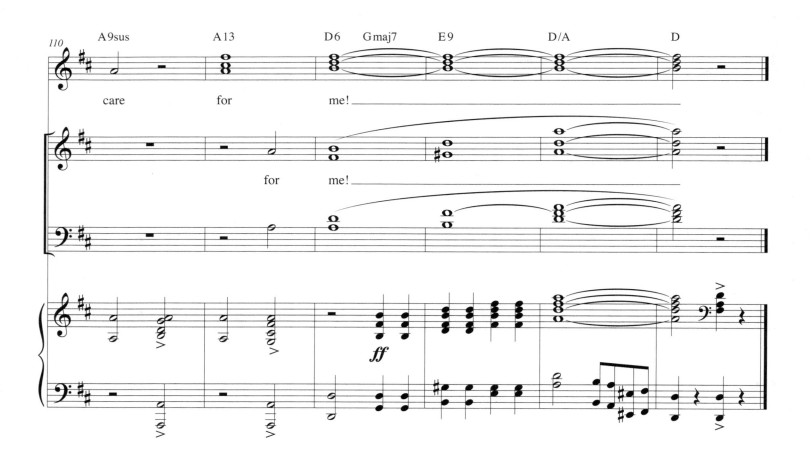

SHALL WE DANCE?

Music and Lyrics by GEORGE GERSHWIN
and IRA GERSHWIN

FIDGETY FEET

Music and Lyrics by GEORGE GERSHWIN
and IRA GERSHWIN

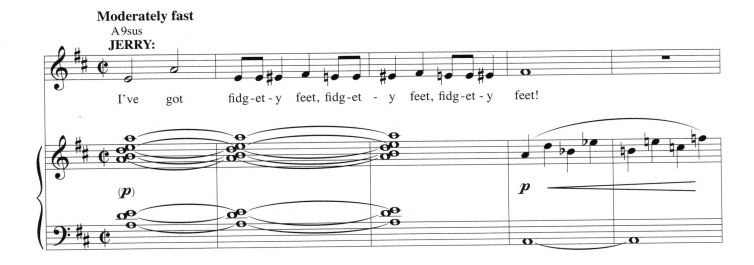

Moderately fast

JERRY:

I've got fidg-et-y feet, fidg-et-y feet, fidg-et-y feet!

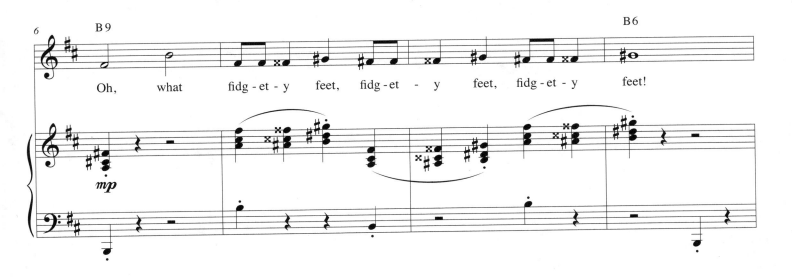

Oh, what fidg-et-y feet, fidg-et-y feet, fidg-et-y feet!

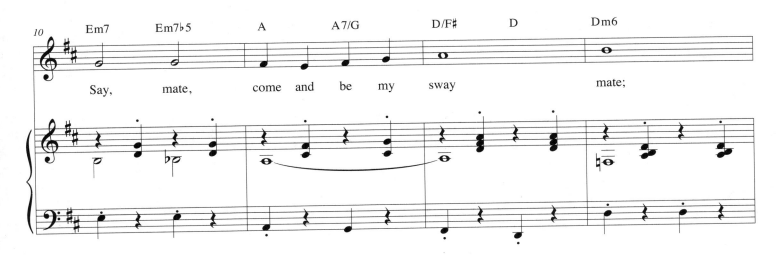

Say, mate, come and be my sway mate;

44

WHO CARES?
(So Long as You Care for Me)

Music and Lyrics by GEORGE GERSHWIN
and IRA GERSHWIN

FOR YOU, FOR ME FOR EVERMORE

Music and Lyrics by GEORGE GERSHWIN
and IRA GERSHWIN

BUT NOT FOR ME

Music and Lyrics by GEORGE GERSHWIN
and IRA GERSHWIN

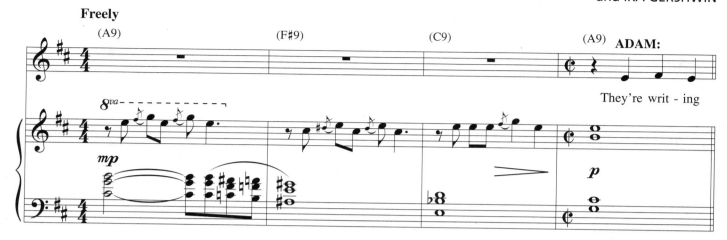

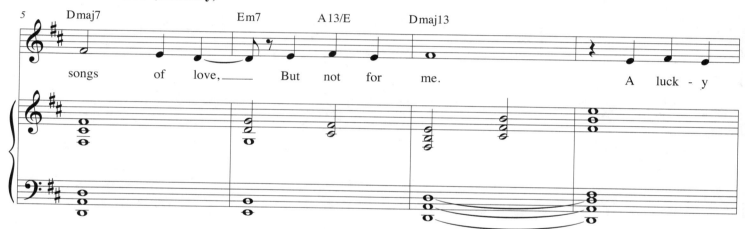

I'LL BUILD A STAIRWAY TO PARADISE

Words by B.G DeSYLVA and IRA GERSHWIN
Music by GEORGE GERSHWIN

Kickline tempo

AN AMERICAN IN PARIS

(Excerpt)

By GEORGE GERSHWIN

Andante ma con ritmo deciso

THEY CAN'T TAKE THAT AWAY FROM ME

Music and Lyrics by GEORGE GERSHWIN
and IRA GERSHWIN

Easy Swing 4